LONELY

LONELY HEARTS

by Gill Adams

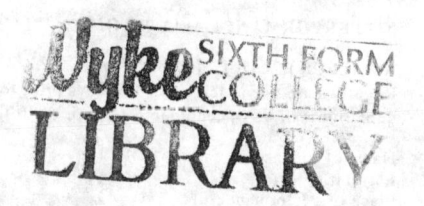

WARNER/CHAPPELL PLAYS

LONDON

A Warner Music Group Company

LONELY HEARTS
First published in 1996
by Warner/Chappell Plays Ltd
129 Park Street, London W1Y 3FA

Copyright © 1995, 1996 by Gill Adams

The author asserts her moral right to be identified as the author of the work.

ISBN 0 85676 218 0

This play is protected by Copyright. According to Copyright Law, no public performance or reading of a protected play or part of that play may be given without prior authorization from Warner/Chappell Plays Ltd., as agent for the Copyright Owners.

From time to time it is necessary to restrict or even withdraw the rights of certain plays. **It is therefore essential to check with us before making a commitment to produce a play.**

NO PERFORMANCE MAY BE GIVEN WITHOUT A LICENCE

AMATEUR PRODUCTIONS
Royalties are due at least fourteen days prior to the first performance. A royalty quotation will be issued upon receipt of the following details:

Name of Licensee
Play Title
Place of Performance
Dates and Number of Performances
Audience Capacity
Ticket Prices

PROFESSIONAL PRODUCTIONS
All enquiries regarding professional rights should be addressed to Warner/Chappell Plays Ltd, 129 Park Street, London W1Y 3FA. Enquiries concerning all others rights should be addressed to A P Watt Ltd, 20 John Street, London WC1N 2DR.

OVERSEAS PRODUCTIONS
Applications for productions overseas should be addressed to our local authorized agents. Further details are listed in our catalogue of plays, published every two years, or available from Warner/Chappell Plays at the address above.

SPECIAL NOTE ON SONGS AND RECORDINGS
For performance of such songs and recordings mentioned in this play as are in copyright, the permission of the copyright owners must be obtained, or other songs and recordings in the public domain substituted.

CONDITIONS OF SALE
This book is sold subject to the condition that it shall not by way of trade or otherwise be re-sold, hired out, circulated or distributed without prior consent of the Publisher. **Reproduction of the text either in whole or part and by any means is strictly forbidden.**

Printed by Commercial Colour Press, London E7

LONELY HEARTS was first presented by Hull Truck Theatre Company at the Hull Truck Theatre, Hull on 5th July, 1995, with the following cast:

RITA   Shaaron Jackson

SILV   Rebecca Clay

BERNIE   Nigel P Betts

BOB   Tim Dantay

Directed by Damian Cruden
Designed by Liam Doona
Lighting designed by Niall Black

LONELY HEARTS was subsequently presented by Hull Truck Theatre Company at the Assembly Rooms, Edinburgh during August 1995 as part of the 1995 Edinburgh Festival.

PROLOGUE

RITA Someone once said to me, "Rita, if you want summat bad enough you'll get it, you've just gotta keep believing . . ." When you've been slimming for nearly twenty years it's hard to believe . . . but do ya know, now I think they was right. Just when you think some things will never change, they do. Some things just get bigger . . . like lies or dreams . . . 'cos let's face it, some things just 'ave to change else we'd go barmy. We was never one's for sitting around and waiting for something to happen, we'd get out there and make it. Alright, sometimes it didn't allus happen straight away . . . and most of the time it didn't allus go right. But one thing's for sure, we allus gave it a bloody good try . . .

ACT ONE

The action takes place in the fitting rooms of two shops, a tailor's and dressmaker's in the present day, and at various times in the past. Upstage centre, the main entrance. Upstage left, a passageway to changing rooms. A few chairs and clothing racks. Around the room are mannequins in various positions. While the scenes often occur independently, the characters remain on stage and the action flows between the two locations, distinguished by changes in lighting.

SILV *and* RITA *in fitting room.* RITA *walks out of a changing room in glasses. She is wearing a partially-fitted wedding dress.*

SILV   Well?

RITA   Well what?

SILV   What do you mean, well what?

RITA   What do you mean "well"? You said . . . well?

SILV   This . . . getting the dress sorted . . . well?

RITA   Am I meant to say summat 'ere? 'Cos if I am just tell me what 'cos I'm buggered if I know . . .

SILV   You're meant to be excited. You're meant to be very excited. You're meant to be summat.

RITA   I'm meant to be a lot of things I'm not. Maybe I'm just me the way I am . . . alright?

SILV   If you say so . . .

RITA   I do.

SILV   Fine.

RITA   Good.

SILV   It smells in here.

RITA   Good . . .

SILV   Moth balls, I reckon.

RITA	Probably.
SILV	(*trying to lighten things*) Mind you, moths don't have balls do they? (*Laughs.*) Oh for fuck's sake Rita, will you crack that bloody face of yours . . .
RITA	(*smiles*) There . . . happy now?
SILV	This is probably summat to do with the seventeen Bacardi and Cokes you downed last night.
RITA	I was sick.
SILV	I'm well aware of that fact, thank you.
RITA	So was you.
SILV	I waited 'till I got indoors.
RITA	(*looking off*) There's half a woman in that dressing room . . .
SILV	I told you Coke was bad for ya . . .
RITA	Well you're good at that aren't ya?
SILV	Good job it was raining.
RITA	It's allus bloody raining!
SILV	'Cos it was all over me mother's front step. Is it the rain?
RITA	Is what the rain?
SILV	You stood there like that . . .
RITA	There's half a woman in that dressing room. Reminds me of someone.
SILV	People say that if you don't get enough sun light it makes you sad or summat.
RITA	That explains it then. (*Picks up the mannequin.*) I'll sit her near the window.
SILV	Or is that just sex? No that's aggressive. I think.

RITA Do ya reckon she came for a fitting an' all?

SILV I know it makes men aggressive.

RITA The rain?

SILV Lack of sex.

RITA Does it?

SILV Definitely.

RITA Bernie's not aggressive, he's soft . . . gentle. He's a very calm sort of bloke. So what's that mean?

SILV It means he must . . . you know . . . when his man's out.

RITA Eh?

SILV You know, 'German Tank' it . . .

RITA Eh?

SILV Forget it . . .

RITA German tank it? (*Suddenly.*) I'm sure he bloody doesn't! I don't think . . .

SILV He must do.

RITA Oh God he probably does all sorts of things I don't know about . . . Oh God, what if he's really weird and I don't know it?

(*A beat.*)

SILV Don't know what?

RITA That my Bernie's a pervert!

SILV Well you'll know soon enough . . . joke! I was joking . . .

RITA I know, but I wasn't. Shit, I'm freezing in this thing.

SILV	It's nerves Rita, it's natural. Bernie's probably just the same.
RITA	What, thinking I'm perverted?
SILV	Nervous.

(*Lights cross fade to* BERNIE *and* BOB, *in the tailor's fitting room.*)

BERNIE	Jesus it's bloody freezing in here!
BOB	Probably 'cos the roof's coming in . . .
BERNIE	It shouldn't take long . . .
BOB	You should have gone to Top Man.
BERNIE	Me mother's sorted it . . . made to measure. Top and tail. He's been doing it for years.
BOB	What, drinking?
BERNIE	He's well known for it.
BOB	Aye, in every pub in town . . .
BERNIE	Look, I promised me mother . . . Rita's having her fitting today . . . now I reckon . . . I bet she looks brilliant in white . . .
BOB	It gives me the creeps.
BERNIE	Eh?
BOB	This place.
BERNIE	I said Rita's bein' fitted up today.
BOB	Like summat out of a Hammer Horror film.
BERNIE	You never listen, do ya?
BOB	(*does an impression of a one-eyed hunchback*) . . . Shit Bernie, 'ave you ever seen the house of wax . . .
BERNIE	See what I mean . . . you never shut up. That was half your problem. 'Cos you never listened, I

never listened. (*To the audience.*) I spent half my life hearing nothing. Nothing but Bob. Me mind was brainwashed. Bob talked at me . . . non-stop he talked at me. But the way it was . . . was wrong. But I believed him. I had to. I had to believe in something. Rita was the only girl I knew who stopped me from not listening.

BOB Bernie, do you ever get the feeling you're being watched?

BERNIE It still raining?

BOB (*indicating the mannequins*) Do ya reckon they base these things on real people?

BERNIE I'm bloody freezing . . .

BOB 'Ere Bernie . . . you ever seen them rubber women?

BERNIE Do you reckon he's alright down there?

BOB I wonder what they're like? (*Looks at* BERNIE.)

BERNIE What? What?

BOB Nowt . . . (*Grins.*) . . . he's probably passed out.

BERNIE Oh God . . . (*To the audience.*) Thing is . . . I was never lucky, see. Never. Rita wasn't lucky either. We wasn't unlucky, we were just not very good at having great things happen to us . . . well, I wasn't. Even when it was possible I never used to see it. Bob was the only one who ever saw anything. He saw it from three streets away, from behind walls . . . he saw things happening even before they happened. He still did whatever he wanted, said whatever he wanted . . . then blamed everyone else. School was years of Bob blaming everyone and everything for every bloody thing that went wrong. School was Bob saying he was a 'doer', but he was no more of a doer than me . . . he was a 'do-nowter' . . . but Bob doing nowt was still summat . . . that was half the problem. Bob did nowt better than anyone else I knew.

(*Music plays — Saturday Night Fever — as the action shifts back to 1976.* BOB *puts white jacket on,* BERNIE *puts platform shoes on.* BERNIE *struts about in just his underpants and high platform shoes. He stands facing the audience as if looking in the mirror. In true John Travolta fashion he moves to the music and combs his hair, etc. He is getting ready for the last school Valentine's disco. Although* BERNIE *tries hard, he's just too small to be cool.* BOB *struts on in John Travolta white suit, super cool. Tall, good looking, and he knows it.* BERNIE *looks at him in disbelief.*)

BERNIE   Shit Bob, where did you find that?

BOB   What?

BERNIE   Suit.

BOB   Dunno.

BERNIE   Dunno?

BOB   (*combing hair*) A bloke does not set out to look for a cool suit, Bernie . . . the suit looks out for a cool bloke.

BERNIE   Wish I'd known . . .

BOB   Just like the chicks, really.

BERNIE   I'd 'ave got one an' all.

BOB   Man, I feel lucky tonight.

BERNIE   Do I look alright?

BOB   (*looking him up and down, keeping him waiting*) Er . . . yeah . . .

BERNIE   Yeah? You sure?

BOB   Yeah, sort of . . .

BERNIE   What does that mean?

BOB	It means get a move on before all the chicks are plucked.
BERNIE	But I look alright? Yeah? Bob? I look alright then? Shoes, shirt an' that . . . yeah?
BOB	I've told ya Bernie. Yes. Just walk six foot behind me. Joke. Come on . . .

(BOB *leads*, BERNIE *follows*. BOB *struts. Very animated, very American. Talks fast, confident. Chews gum. Casual, yet on edge. Looking around for action.* BERNIE *half runs, half walks, hanging on* BOB'S *every word*.)

Ya see Bernie, life is full of the do-ers and the don't-ers. I personally am a doer. I get in there and I do. Right? Where you Bernie, no offence intended, but you are a don't-er . . . you don't get in and you don't do. See? See what I'm saying here? Most blokes are dick dribblers, Bernie . . . They take one look at a chick and their eyes are out on sticks, man, their tongues are hanging . . . No respect. No style. See Jackson, right? His big ambition in life is to jack in some chick's face . . . call that ambition? Call that respect? Na. Ya see Bernie, Jackson has got no fuckin' style . . . no fuckin' respect and he ain't a do-er, see.

(BOB *and* BERNIE *stand, looking around*.)

This place is easy pickings mate. No problem. Easy.

BERNIE	So where are all these chicks then?
BOB	Early doors Bernie. Early doors . . .

(*Throughout this scene*, SILV *does not look at* BOB *and* BOB *does not look at* SILV. *They each use* BERNIE *and* RITA *to do their spying*.)

SILV	So?
RITA	Yeah.

SILV	Sure?
RITA	Yeah, it's them . . . yeah even without me specks I can see it's definitely them. It's Bob's suit, I think it's fluorescent.
BOB	Well?
BERNIE	Yeah it's them.
BOB	They looking then?
BERNIE	No . . . yes . . . no.
BOB	Don't let 'em see ya.
RITA	I think they've seen us . . .
SILV	You sure?
RITA	Yeah . . .
SILV	Well don't let 'em see you're looking. Well?
BERNIE	What?
BOB	They coming over here or what?
RITA	No.
SILV	No?
RITA	No.
SILV	What you doing?
RITA	What's it look like . . .
SILV	Put 'em away!
RITA	It always works.
SILV	Rita, put 'em away. Jesus! There's more to being a woman then 'aving a big pair of tits.
RITA	Like what?
SILV	Eh?
RITA	What else?

SILV	Oh shurrup.
BERNIE	Why don't we . . .
RITA	Just go and talk to 'em?
SILV	Don't keep staring!
BOB	Ignore 'em for a bit.
SILV	Have a quick look. Just a quick 'un though.
BOB	Well? Are they coming yet?
BERNIE	Na . . .
RITA	Na . . .
SILV	Shit.
BOB	Fuck.
RITA	Can't we just . . . you know, walk past or summat?
BERNIE	Real casual like . . . ignoring 'em completely?
SILV	Yeah.
BOB	Alright . . .

(*They all four move together.*)

SILV	Don't stare.
BOB	Try not to trip in them bloody shoes.

(*They walk right past each other.*)

SILV	Shit, did he look?
RITA	Shall we do it again?
SILV	Well?
RITA	(*well bored by now*) Nope.
BOB	They looking?
BERNIE	Nope.

SILV	Look again . . . well?
	(RITA *just shakes her head.*)
BOB	Look again . . .
	(BERNIE *just shakes his head.*)
SILV	Shit.
RITA	You're telling me it's shit, it's more than shit — it's piss an' all. Everyone's got someone except us.
SILV	Oh shurrup moaning, Rita.
RITA	Well it's true!
BOB	I don't understand it, man . . .
BERNIE	(*laughs*) Maybe it's that suit, maybe it's blinding 'em!
BOB	Maybe it's your bleedin' mug.
BERNIE	Why don't we just get in there? You know, be a do-er?
BOB	Why don't you just shut it?
RITA	I don't mind going up to 'em and just asking . . .
SILV	(*snaps*) ASKING WHAT?
RITA	For a dance an' that . . .
SILV	Rita we've been here nearly all frigging night and they ain't so much as looked our way . . . summat's wrong . . . (*She looks critically at* RITA.)
RITA	What? What you looking at me like that for?
BERNIE	Why don't I just go over, ya know, dead casual and bump into the big one, Rita, and well, you know ask her like . . .
BOB	Ask 'er like what?

BERNIE	Well . . .
BOB	Oh shurrup . . . five more minutes and I'm off.
SILV	I'll give 'em two more minutes then we're going . . . right, come on!
RITA	EH! That weren't two minutes, that weren't even one! Wait . . . SILV!

(SILV *walks off in the other direction*.)

BOB	I'm out of 'ere. Chicks . . . they do my 'ead in . . .

(BOB *also walks off. Music plays, How Deep is Your Love, by the Bee Gees.* BERNIE *and* RITA *find themselves alone together. They begin to dance.*)

RITA	Why does everything have to change?
BERNIE	(*back in time*) Dunno. It just does.
RITA	What about inside?
BERNIE	Inside where?
RITA	Us.
BERNIE	Head?
RITA	Heart. (*She pulls his hand near her heart.*)
BERNIE	Shit!
RITA	You dance really different.
BERNIE	I practice in front of the mirror . . . but it's only small, I can't see what me feet are doing . . . Rita . . .
RITA	Bernie.
BERNIE	Bob's gone.
RITA	Good.
BERNIE	I've got to go . . . soon. In a bit . . . when I feel like it . . . shit . . . I might stay 'till the end, even.

RITA	This is the end.
BERNIE	Is it?
RITA	The last dance . . .

(*The music stops and the lights change, back to the changing room and the present.*)

SILV	Last chance . . .
RITA	Yeah . . .
SILV	Everything changed though.
RITA	I know . . . why does everything have to change?
BERNIE	Do ya know Rita was the only girl I ever danced with. I'm not one for dancing.
BOB	It's the feet. I don't think they're connected to that part of the body that's supposed to move to the music.
BERNIE	True. Above the knees I'm fine. Below the knees I'm a sort of stand still and shuffle sort of dancer.
BOB	Look, if the top half's busy then they don't notice what's going on below. I've always thought throwing your arms about's a good distraction . . .
BERNIE	(*to the audience, aside*) I hated the Bee Gees. But when I danced with Rita it was like the music was in me head . . . it was mine, something that I'd saved . . . I was dancing to me own rhythm . . . I was dancing below the knees.
RITA	I was thinking about Bernie.
SILV	Ain't it gone quiet? Shit, this place gives me the creeps.
RITA	At school.
SILV	It's stopped raining.
RITA	Nothing mattered then, did it?

SILV	Mind you it's forecast on and off all day . . . typical.
RITA	He was a terrible dancer.
SILV	What do you mean was?
RITA	Trouble is, he sweats so much I think it puts him off being too physical.
SILV	I've always thought sex in a shower must be nice. Clean but dead mucky.
RITA	His feet don't work properly . . . he just moves his chin a lot.

(*Lights change. Back to the disco, back in time.*)

BERNIE	Oh I was just getting the hang of it and all.
RITA	I can't believe you've left school . . .
BERNIE	That's what me mam says . . . I mean . . . yeah I know . . . it's hot in 'ere isn't it?
RITA	The music stopped.
BERNIE	Has it? Oh yeah . . . once I start I can't stop. It's the feet . . . STOP! (*Looks down.*) STOP DANCING!
RITA	Do ya want to walk me home?
BERNIE	I . . . it's just, I promised Bob — he leaves for the Army . . . yeah.

(*The lights change.* BERNIE *is walking* RITA *home.*)

RITA	You joining the army, like Bob?
BERNIE	Dunno, might do . . . might not. I've got more choice than Bob, see. I could go into business . . .
RITA	Business?
BERNIE	Yeah . . . dunno yet . . . ain't made me mind up . . .

RITA I wish I was leaving school an' all . . . I'd go into business. Hair dressing or beautician, summat like that. Does Bob like Silv?

BERNIE Bob likes no one much . . .

RITA 'Cept 'imself right? (*Laughs.*)

BERNIE Yeah right . . . (*He laughs, then is suddenly embarrassed.*)

RITA I hope you don't join the army, I couldn't stand the thought of you being blown to pieces. (*Smiles.*) Joke.

BERNIE Well yeah, there is that I suppose. (*Suddenly thinks about this.*) Shit . . .

RITA Silv likes him loads . . . she likes him . . . loads I think.

BERNIE Shit . . . fancy bein' blown to pieces!

RITA She even likes them awful suits he wears . . .

BERNIE Mind you, I think they have to train you up for ages first. You know, 'till you get good enough an' that.

RITA What, good enough to be blown to pieces? (*Laughs.*)

BERNIE (*laughs*) Yeah. Look, I'd better get off. Bob'll be wondering where I am an' that . . . he leaves Monday.

RITA Monday? I better tell Silv . . . Bernie?

BERNIE (*slightly distracted*) What?

RITA (*brief pause, then suddenly*) Don't join the army will ya? I'd go into business if I was you, I can see you with a briefcase.

(*The lights change. Back to the fitting room.*)

BERNIE	Rita was the first person that ever said summat would suit me.
BOB	These trousers he's meant to be making.
BERNIE	What about 'em?
BOB	They're not flares are they? (*Laughs.*)
BERNIE	(*to the audience*) Bob always had away of spoiling things . . . it weren't his fault it was his mouth.

(*Back in time.* BOB, *on edge, sits on his own. He's drinking from a bottle.*)

BERNIE	Where you been?
BOB	The thing about chicks Bernie is they are seriously weird.
BERNIE	Bob I've been thinking . . . you could always come into business with me . . . on the round an' that . . . partners.
BOB	Take that Silv . . . God was cruel to her, Bernie. Gave her a great face . . . great body, but a fuckin' weird personality.
BERNIE	We could get a van an' that . . . put our names down the side, the lot?
BOB	And her fat friend. (*Laughs.*) Man, she is one weird desperate chick, someone should do her one big favour. Put a sack over her face and give her one. (*He sees* BERNIE'S *face react.*)
BERNIE	Can I have a drink of that?
BOB	'Ere, share an' share alike, that's what mates are for. (*Passes bottle.*)
SILV	I know who he left with, Rita. The Bucket.
RITA	I know. She was hanging around the doors, begging for it.

SILV   See that's typical of a fella. They only want one thing.

RITA   True.

SILV   They're all the bloody same.

RITA   True. Can I have a drink?

SILV   Well army or no army he's welcome to her,

RITA   She's easy . . . Silv? Can I have a drink now?

(SILV *passes her a bottle.*)

SILV   'Ere, I'm not bothered any road. Jackson was givin' it loads. He's fancied me for ages. He's had his ear pierced an' all. Was wearing a stud. Mind you it looked a bit septic . . .

RITA   He should use salt and water.

SILV   Well I'm glad he's leaving.

RITA   Or Detol. TCP even . . . mind you . . . (*Takes a big swig, nearly chokes.*)

SILV   What's the point in lovin' someone in the bloody army?

RITA   It stinks.

SILV   (*takes bottle back*) You're tellin' me. No, he can get lost . . .

RITA   Or be blown to bits.

SILV   Shit . . . do ya think they're doing it?

RITA   Eh?

(*Lights change.*)

BOB   I reckon she's with Jackson.

BERNIE Dunno.

BOB   Both of 'em.

BERNIE	Eh?
BOB	Jackson and his brother.
BERNIE	No . . .
BOB	That fat one'll be begging for it.
BERNIE	With Jackson?
BOB	Yeah she'll have them flabby tits out . . .
BERNIE	With Jackson?
BOB	Jackson milking her dry . . .
BERNIE	Shit, Jackson?

(*Lights change.*)

SILV	And his side-kick'll be with her spotty friend.
RITA	Bernie?
SILV	They stick together like glue, them two . . . pathetic.
RITA	What, Bernie and spotty Sue?
SILV	I bet he's well sick he can't get into the army.
RITA	He can.
SILV	He can't stupid, he's too soft . . .

(*Lights change.*)

BOB	Shit Bernie, I've gotta get laid before Monday. I promised meself.
BERNIE	Bob?
BOB	What?
BERNIE	Aren't you frightened? You know, 'bout movin' away an' that . . . joining the army.
BOB	Frightened? I was born to be a soldier Bernie. This time next week I'll be in Germany, man.

	Where will you be? Up a frigging ladder washing winda's . . .
BERNIE	But what if there's another war?

(*Lights change.*)

SILV	I should have smacked the slag.
RITA	Yeah, and gone straight up to him and said, "Bob. I fancy ya. You're joining the army. I'm stayin' here. You might get blown to pieces, I might get run over by . . . (*Takes another big swig.*) . . . a double-decker bus . . . we're free . . . and randy. Come 'ere and give me one".
SILV	Oh shurrup, Rita. (*Grabs bottle back.*)

(*Lights change.*)

BOB	See this suit Bernie, come Monday mate, it's yours!
BERNIE	(*down*) Great.
BOB	'Course you'll have to lose a bit of weight first. Joke. No, seriously mate, it's yours . . . drives women wild, this suit.
BERNIE	Well it didn't do you much good tonight, did it?
BOB	What you trying to say?
BERNIE	It didn't do you much good . . . that's all.
BOB	You, Bernie, have got one serious fucking problem, mate. You shit outta your mouth. (*Walks off suddenly.*) Me. Next week. Army. Germany. Uniform. Soldier, right? Right! Yes Sir! You the rest of your miserable life. Up a friggin' ladder.
BERNIE	(*shouting after him*) The suit is shit, Bob.

(*Lights change.*)

SILV	You sexy thing.
RITA	I know . . . (*Grins.*)

SILV	Stupid, the song . . .
RITA	I like "Jive Talking".
SILV	I like "Dancing in the Street".
RITA	When?
SILV	I'm still waiting.
RITA	For Bob?
SILV	By Diana Ross . . .
RITA	(*sings*) I'll be there . . .
SILV	You allus bloody are, that's half the problem.
RITA	I wonder who'll be me first . . .
SILV	Some poor sod.
RITA	(*sings*) What becomes of the broken-hearted . . .
SILV	I feel sick . . .
RITA	It allus makes me cry . . .
SILV	I think I'm gonna puke . . .
RITA	(*sings*) Take a good look at my face . . . breaks me heart.
SILV	Oh God . . .
RITA	Don't know why.
SILV	Oh God I'm gonna chuck, Reet. I think it's . . .
RITA	The words?
SILV	The cider . . .

(*Lights change, to take in both scenes at once.*)

BOB	If you're lucky you'll get a girl — get 'er up the duff — get married and live a miserable bleedin' life. True.

BERNIE	That suit is not cool, Bob.
SILV	Oh, God the room's spinning, Reet.
RITA	We're outside . . .
BOB	Up a friggin' ladder . . .
RITA	I wonder if hurts . . . the first time.
SILV	Oh shurrup.
RITA	Pauline Saunders told me that when she did it in the bath with Kevin Fisher the water turned bright red . . . ya know, blood an' stuff . . . ugh . . .
SILV	Rubbish.
RITA	She walked funny for weeks.
SILV	Bollocks.
RITA	Mind you she allus did.
SILV	Oh shurrup.
RITA	He packed her in the next day. (*Beat.*) Slag. I bet you do it first.
SILV	'Course I will.
RITA	I daren't . . . me mam'll kill me.
SILV	She won't know, stupid.
RITA	'Course she will. Mothers know everything, anyway you change, all of a sudden you change . . . you look different . . . more grown up.
SILV	Guilty . . .
RITA	Special.
SILV	Scared.
RITA	Up the duff . . . joke.
	(*Pause.*)

SILV   Oh shurrup Rita. God, cider don't half make me feel sick.

RITA   Soft lighting . . . nice music . . . candles . . . I like the Bee Gees, don't you?

SILV   Bee Gees make me sick.

RITA   Barry White.

SILV   Hot Chocolate.

RITA   Na, posh wine . . . chilled . . .

SILV   Oh God, the world's spinning Reet . . .

BERNIE   (*shouts*) The suit is shit, Bob.

(*Loud guitar. Drums and repeated beat comes in wild and furious, from 'Schools Out' by Alice Cooper.* BERNIE *dances. Then back to the present.*)

RITA   (*to the audience*) That night, the night of the last Valentine's disco, everything changed. Bob left for the army, Bernie moved to the other end of town with his mother . . . and Silv lost her virginity, burned the bus shelter down and got caught . . . not just burning the shelter down, but pregnant. Bob never knew . . . Bernie never knew. Let's face it, I didn't even know, not for ages. Don't know why she didn't tell me . . . she's always told me everything. But I dunno, that night changed us all. Like something just snapped. Nowt could ever be the same again.

SILV   'Ere Rita. Sort us out, will ya? Me chain's caught in me hair . . . what you still sat there for?

RITA   I was thinking 'bout something.

BERNIE   You know that night before you left for the army?

BOB   (*snaps*) What you on about that for? Bernie, the past is the past . . . forget it.

BERNIE   Why did you burn it down?

BOB	What?
BERNIE	Bus shelter.
SILV	Rita . . . are you happy?
RITA	Yeah.
SILV	Then forget the past.
RITA	It don't make sense . . .
SILV	Shit, we've still got loads to do, and you lady have still gotta get that mop sorted.
RITA	Why did you burn it down?
SILV	Rita if you don't get a move on, the hairdressers'll be shut. (*Pause.*) There was nowt to tell. He set fire to it, it burnt down.
RITA	Just like that?
SILV	Yeah just like that.
RITA	He could have lost everything . . .
SILV	He deserved to lose everything . . . I did. He did it. It was 'is fault . . .
RITA	This dress is driving me mad. It's itching like mad. (*She struggles.*)
SILV	Don't do that Rita . . . you'll rip it. Now look what you've done!
BOB	It's still pissing it down outside. Racing'll be a joke.
BERNIE	Racing is a joke.
BOB	Only for you 'cause you always lose, mate.
BERNIE	And you always win right?
BOB	Sometimes . . . most of the time. Yeah.
BERNIE	You just think you win.

BOB   Bernie, I'm not being personal or owt, but I find it a bit hard to take you serious when you're sat there in just your under-crackers, son . . . alright?

BERNIE   See what I mean?

BOB   So I put my money on to win . . . I'm a first place sort of bloke. You can't stand it cause you're not the same as me. "I'll take anything but first place" . . . that's you.

RITA   Don't you ever stare at yourself until the world disappears and all you can see are two eyes staring at you . . . eyes you don't even recognise . . .

SILV   (*sarcastic*) Oh aye Reet, all the time . . .

RITA   Does it not bother you?

SILV   Does what not bother me?

RITA   The unknown.

SILV   I tell what does bother me — you going all deep on me . . . lighten up, Reet. God I'm gagging for a drink.

RITA   It bothers me . . .

SILV   I know, maybe I should nip to beer-off shop, get some cans.

RITA   I look at meself sometimes and think, who is this fat person? Inside I'm not fat . . . I look at this body and it feels all wrong. Like I'm carrying someone else's. This fat's not mine.

SILV   This is you worrying about fitting into this dress, in't it? Rita . . . it's natural. This dress is gonna fit you like a glove, made to measure, it'll move with you, it'll look like a second skin. It's my hair I'm worried about . . . just look at this hair Reet, is this a state or what?

RITA   I'm not happy with me body.

SILV	Don't worry. Even in marriage it's not compulsory to stand totally bare-arsed in front of your husband.
RITA	Bernie's body and mine are the same.
SILV	I sincerely hope not.
RITA	We both feel trapped inside summat that's not ours . . . I know he feels the same. I can tell by the way he moves.
SILV	Rita I don't think these are positive thoughts. I think maybe OK, these are thoughts that have a slight, and I mean slight grain of truth in 'em, but I really think you should stop thinking 'em . . . any road, half your problem's water retention.
RITA	True, if women pissed like horses we'd all be size ten.

(*Lights change.* BOB *is messing about with the mannequins.*)

BOB	"Oh Bernard, not again . . . put your jim-jams back on and go to sleep". Women, Bernie, are all the same. They say they will, they even look like they will, but when it comes down to it they won't. It's a habit they have.
BERNIE	All women are not the same, Bob. All women are definitely all different. I hate when you start all that "Women Bernie are all the bloody same" routine. I don't want to hear it no more, Bob. Women are not all the same. Rita is not like Silv, you know it and I know it . . . they know it. Alright?
BOB	Touch . . . y. I think I sense a few nerves building up 'ere . . . I think there is a definite smell of fear in this here changing room, don't you?
RITA	Do you really think the way we look is important?
SILV	When?

RITA	All the time. I mean is this what people really see? (*Looking at herself.*)
SILV	'Course it is?
RITA	No I mean really . . .
SILV	Yeah . . . what do you mean?
RITA	But is this the real us? This reflection.
SILV	Oh I don't know.
RITA	I can't stand to be mauled. Stood half naked and have someone fiddling about with me. I wish I'd gone for one already made. I feel fat. I am fat. Oh God, I look demented in white.
BERNIE	Do you think I'm sexy?
BOB	Eh?
BERNIE	From a woman's point of view.
BOB	Whose?
BERNIE	Well . . . Rita's.
BOB	What you trying to say?
BERNIE	Nowt . . . are you cold?

(BOB *looks at* BERNIE'S *legs, etc.*)

BOB	I think you might need to see if this bloke's still alive, son. Waiting like this is turning you strange.
BERNIE	You're so full of shit Bob.
BOB	See what I mean? Don't push it sunshine. (*Taking the piss.*) Bob, do you think I'm sexy? Shit . . . that is a gem. That's a joke.
BERNIE	So, I'm a joke am I?
BOB	I need some fresh air, it stinks of stale under-crackers in 'ere.

BERNIE My underpants are clean on every day, Bob. Unlike you Bob, I have someone looking after me. Now I have two. Rita and me mother.

BOB I used to back this horse, Bernie. I put money on it cause I believed it was gonna run its tail off for me . . . out of all the horses in the world, I'd back that one. But then one day it doesn't even get over the line. It just gives up. You remind me of that horse, Bernie.

SILV We never really tell each other the truth, do we?

RITA Us?

SILV People.

RITA What people?

SILV No one . . . aren't things that are half-made weird . . .

RITA Dress?

SILV Life . . . mine was half-made for years. Bob gone. Baby inside me . . . half-made . . . then fully made, ready to come out. Who tells it to . . . I mean really? How does it know?

RITA Babies just know. I think they must do.

(*Lights change. Back in time. The song This Old Heart of Mine, by Rod Stewart plays to fade.* SILV *is heavily pregnant.*)

RITA What do you reckon he's doing right now?

SILV Who?

RITA Rod Stewart.

SILV How should I know . . . with some model probably . . .

RITA Na, he's at his luxury hotel waiting for me.

SILV	To fall out of the wardrobe and be carted off by security.
RITA	He might be on stage. What do you reckon?
SILV	I don't know and frankly Rita I don't care . . . My belly's killing me . . . I think it was them pilchards.
RITA	We could pretend.
SILV	Pretend what? That your not barmy and I'm not . . . (*Looks down.*) Fat?
RITA	That we're there at the concert . . . right up the front, special seats. VIPs . . . and Rod's looking into me eyes and singing just to me . . .
SILV	With six hundred hysterical lasses all kickin' your face in.
RITA	Well I can't help it if he loves only me . . .
SILV	Oh shit . . .
RITA	(*in a world of her own*) After the show he showers. I pass him a towel, he lets me pat him dry . . . pat . . . pat . . .
SILV	(*doubled up now*) Oh God . . .
RITA	I dry his whole body . . . every inch . . . 'course he can hardly control himself, he wants me . . . desperately . . .
SILV	Oh fuck, Rita!
RITA	Eh? Give him a chance!
SILV	I think it's bloody well coming.
RITA	Eh? (*Grinning.*)
SILV	Give over Rita . . . I'm in bloody agony 'ere!
RITA	It's called ecstasy Silv. I've read about it in Cosmo'.
SILV	It's called pain, Rita . . . me mam's warned me . . .

RITA	Pain and pleasure, that's what love is all about . . .
SILV	I can't breathe. I've forgot how to breathe!
RITA	Neither can I . . . oh Rod, I love you . . .
SILV	Oh Rita will you shut the fuck up and . . . oh shit . . . I think I've peed meself!
RITA	(*looks at her very seriously*) My God Silv, I think you've just experienced an orgasm!
SILV	My God Rita, I've just experienced me bloody waters breaking . . . oh no. I wish me mother was 'ere!
RITA	What you trying to say?
SILV	I'm 'avin' it, you stupid dozy cow!
RITA	What, now?
SILV	YES!
RITA	But you're at home.
SILV	You don't say! Oh God!
RITA	Oh God.
SILV	SHIT!
RITA	Oh shit.
SILV	Stop repeating everything I say . . . oh God. I want me mam.
RITA	So do I.
SILV	She's at bingo . . . it's the gold rush tonight, twenty grand — she'll go barmy if she misses it.
RITA	Twenty grand? Blimey!
SILV	I want me mam!
RITA	Oh shit, look where's them magazines you've been buying?

SILV	What for?
RITA	Instructions.
SILV	Oh God . . .
RITA	Shall I boil the kettle?
SILV	Shall I boil your head?
RITA	Well what then? What shall I do?
SILV	I don't know . . . I want me mam.
RITA	Shall I ring the police?
SILV	RING THE ARMY!
RITA	The army?
SILV	I miss him, Rita.
RITA	Who? Bob? Oh shit . . . shall I ring for an ambulance?
SILV	NO. SING.
RITA	Sing?
SILV	Sing 'till me mam comes home.
RITA	I don't know that one . . .
SILV	Oh God . . . please help me.
RITA	Oh don't cry Silv, you'll set me off . . .
SILV	When I was poorly me mam always sang to me . . . Michael row the boat ashore . . .
RITA	That's nice . . .
SILV	Ugh . . . God . . . sing summat Rita . . . sing summat quick!
RITA	I'm thinking . . . do ya want summat out the top ten?
SILV	Anything . . . sing anything.

(RITA *jumps up. A piano intro plays, and she sings dramatically 'I Will Survive', by Gloria Gaynor.*)

RITA (*singing*) At first I was afraid, I was petrified . . .

SILV Oh God help me!

RITA (*louder*) Kept thinking I could never live without you by my side. But then I spent so many nights thinking how you did me wrong, and I grew strong, and I learnt how to get along . . . and so you're back . . .

(*The music stops and the lights change back to the present.*)

SILV No one should have the right to take summat from someone without them wanting it . . . should they?

RITA You couldn't keep her, you was too young . . . messed up in your mind. You didn't want her, Silv.

SILV I'm not talking about the baby.

BERNIE Seventeen years in the army messed you up, Bob . . . admit it, you hated it.

BOB What would you know?

BERNIE Stop treating me like I'm an idiot Bob. I know what I've seen and I've seen what the army did to you. We're mates. I care. I always did. It's just hard to care for you sometimes, 'cos your such an arsehole.

BOB Army was all I wanted.

(*Lights change. Back in time.* BOB *is just out of the army,* BERNIE *is cool with him.*)

BOB I'm out Bernie. Out for good. Germany, army. Jack shit.

BERNIE   So you're out . . . what did you want, a street party?

BOB   I expected a bit more than this, yeah.

BERNIE   Who from? Me?

BOB   Why, is that a problem, is it?

BERNIE   No.

BOB   But you don't wanna know, right?

BERNIE   I never said that.

BOB   Some mate. I've been out three weeks.

BERNIE   I've changed.

BOB   What's that mean . . . "I've changed".

BERNIE   It means I'm not the same Bernie I was at school, alright?

BOB   You're telling me. No it's true. I noticed straight away. Bob, I thought . . . Bernie has changed. In all these years he's grown . . . fatter. (*Laughs.*)

BERNIE   But you're just the same.

BOB   Jesus Bernie, you lost your sense of humour or what?

BERNIE   No Bob. I just no longer find it funny when you take the piss. Strange that, isn't it. I wonder why that could be. I wonder if it's because you've been so far away from me I've got used to feeling like I count for summat. Summat more than just a dummy for you to have crack at. What do you think?

BOB   Hey that's cool with me. No, I mean it Bernie. I look around and I can see you've changed. Developed . . . advanced, maybe even prospered a little. (*Suddenly angry.*) WELL FUCK YOU!

(*Pause.*)

BERNIE   And you haven't changed one bit . . .

BOB   Oh you're wrong. You are very . . . wrong. But what's it matter, eh? What's it to you? I looked you up, and you didn't even crack your friggin' face. You ask me . . . nothing, like why I'm out? What the fuck I've been doing all these years . . . like what the fuck am I gonna do now. You couldn't give a shit.

BERNIE   You've a short memory Bob.

BOB   I must have 'cos I used to think you were a decent mate.

BERNIE   You got in the army. Great. You was a god. Bob Chapman. Army. Germany. Soldier. That last night. You in your friggin' cool suit . . . out to pull the chicks . . . I'm off Monday, fuck everyone else. Fuck you, Bernie.

BOB   You make me piss meself. Look at ya. Little van, little ladder, little fuckin' bucket . . . little fuckin' life. Tell me summat Bernie . . . when you're going up and down them little ladders all day do ya whistle to yourself? Do ya whistle while you work?

BERNIE   Sometimes.

BOB   No letter. No nowt. I wrote. I rang. Bernie has moved they told me. Moved with his mother to the other side of town . . . Great I thought. Brilliant. Bernie has moved . . .

BERNIE   That night, I came and asked you straight . . . did you or didn't you . . .

BOB   I never said it was Rita . . .

BERNIE   You don't know what friendship means.

BOB   So all this is about what? Some fat lass at school, right?

BERNIE   I've nowt to say to you Bob.

BOB But we've been mates years, Bernie. Years . . .

BERNIE I've nowt to say to you Bob.

BOB So that's it then? Eh? The big man has spoken?

BERNIE Yes.

BOB This is all over one daft lass . . .

BERNIE No.

BOB Fat Rita.

BERNIE YOU HAD 'EM BOTH, RITA AND SILV. TWO IN ONE NIGHT, REMEMBER?

BOB It was a lie. It's what blokes do. They fuck up. They lie. You knew it wasn't true? I fucked up. I lied. I'm sorry . . . I just didn't want to leave like a loser . . . that's all.

(*Pause.*)

BERNIE I knew it wasn't true.

(*Lights change. Back to the present day.*)

BERNIE 'Ere . . . (*Offers him some gum.*) Sun's out. Racing'll be on this afternoon, I reckon . . . do you think about her still?

BOB Who?

BERNIE Your mam.

BOB No. I fancy summat in the 2:30. How much dosh you got?

BERNIE Funny . . .

BOB (*looking out the window*) It's probably gonna piss it down again.

BERNIE Probably.

BOB This room reminds me of summat.

BERNIE   What?

BOB   A morgue.

SILV   I wish you'd sit down, you're making me nervous.

RITA   I feel trapped. I can't breathe in this thing. Silv, I don't think Bernie loves me. I just think he was lonely.

SILV   What about cupid's bloody arrow? And fate?

RITA   It was rubbish.

SILV   It came true.

RITA   I was just bored, wasn't I? Well, maybe Bernie was the same?

SILV   Bernie has always been bored. He's never done owt amazing. Bob's allus stopping him. Him deciding to look for someone was probably the most exciting idea he's ever had in his life.

RITA   But what about me?

SILV   What about you?

RITA   Am I alright? I mean really?

SILV   (*laughs*) 'Course you're alright . . . you was looking for someone special . . . summat new. You wanted summat to happen, that's all. Packing peas all night. Sleeping nearly all day . . . waiting at bus stops is not 'having a great life', is it? You wanted to change, Rita . . . you was brave. You made a decision and stuck to it . . .

RITA   Really.

SILV   Oh shurrup, barmy . . . we was bored. I was bored. Our friggin' life was as dull as it gets.

RITA   "Date Mate!"

SILV   The small ads that change people's lives.

RITA By Valentine's Day we were both supposed to be with the men we were going to marry.

SILV Rita . . .

RITA What?

SILV Wake up . . . grow up and please shut up, alright?

BERNIE Blind dates are weird.

BOB So?

BERNIE They are though. All I mean. No exceptions. Everyone's a one hundred percent round the friggin' bend weird person . . . I've just realised . . . everyone had massive hang-ups . . . huge personality defects . . . everyone was desperate.

BOB Yeah.

BERNIE So what does that make me? And Rita, what does that make Rita?

BOB Bernie, I think you may be panicking a bit 'ere.

BERNIE We must be the same . . . we must be . . .

BOB Bernie. You just was a window cleaner who wanted someone to go out with . . . you don't have a personality problem . . . it's called being shy, that's all. You was looking for a bit of excitement. It's understandable. I gamble. You stay in and watch telly with your mam. I pick up lasses. Don't care what they look like, I pick 'em up, I give 'em one. You don't. That's all. End of story. So drop it, right?

BERNIE I wish you'd sit down. You're making me nervous.

RITA I wonder where ideas come from, I mean really — who put's 'em in our heads and why do we believe in them? Do ya reckon it was 'im?

SILV Who you on about now?

RITA	Cupid? Sat on his cloud aiming his arrow at my heart.
SILV	Arse more like.
RITA	I wonder if he's got it out now?
SILV	Probably, dirty bastard.
RITA	'Ere, he might be aiming it at you.
SILV	Do ya think it's stopped raining? I might nip to shops . . .

(*Lights change.* BOB *is looking up at the stars.*)

BOB	See them stars, Bernie? They're a con.
BERNIE	A con? What do you mean a con?
BOB	They're there to con you into believing in summat more . . .
BERNIE	More than what?
BOB	Blackness.
BERNIE	No.
BOB	(*grabbing* BERNIE'S *face and holding it up towards the sky*) Look beyond the stars, Bernie. What do ya see?
BERNIE	The sky . . .
BOB	Try again.
BERNIE	It's the sky.
BOB	What colour is it?
BERNIE	It's just the sky at night . . .
BOB	What colour is it?
BERNIE	It's just dark, that's all.
BOB	(*holds his head tighter*) What's beyond the fucking stars Bernie, open your eyes and take a proper look!

BERNIE	Black . . . ness.
BOB	(*letting go*) Thank you.

(*Lights change. Back to the fitting room.*)

BOB	What's that face for now?
BERNIE	You . . .
BOB	So it's my fault is it?
BERNIE	You can't keep it shut, can you . . . not even today, not even tomorrow . . . you have to open that bitter mouth of yours and try to spoil it, don't ya?
BOB	Tell me summat Bernie . . . tell me summat. Just to save Rita from becoming a widow before she's even a wife . . . are we here for me or you?
BERNIE	You said wife . . .

(BOB *holds out one of the mannequins and nuts it.*)

BOB	This old twat downstairs. If he's not dead already, I'm gonna kill him.
BERNIE	It was meant to be . . . it was destiny.
BOB	It was fucking insanity . . .
BERNIE	We were made for each other.

(*Back to* SILV *and* RITA.)

RITA	What is happiness. I mean really . . . laughing in't happiness, is it?
SILV	But Bernie makes you happy don't he? You was obsessed.
RITA	I was not. I was just determined.
SILV	Well what ever you call it you nearly drove me round the bend . . .

(*Lights change. Back in time.*)

RITA	Right I'm ready . . .
SILV	Ready? For what?
RITA	To write me replies. It's make me mind up time . . .
SILV	You are joking?
RITA	No.
SILV	You're really gonna risk meeting one of 'em?
RITA	'Course I am.
SILV	Your barmy.
RITA	You can choose one an' all.
SILV	Oh yeah. I'll have the one with the speech impediment and halitosis . . .
RITA	That's cruel.
SILV	But true.
RITA	You don't know that.
SILV	Oh I do.
RITA	Maybe there's just one who's right, eh? Why don't you 'ave a look?
SILV	For you maybe . . . just leave me out of it.
RITA	I think they're all just a bit lonely really.
SILV	That bloke in Silence of the Lambs was just a bit lonely.
RITA	What if he's just unlucky in love?
SILV	In other words, pathetic.
RITA	What if he's shy?
SILV	With a nervous twitch, club foot and withered hand?
RITA	So.

SILV   So go out with a freak then . . .

(*Lights change.* BOB *and* BERNIE *sitting in the pub.* BERNIE *holds a pen and has the local paper opened to the "Date Mate" section.*)

BOB   So you're putting another in then?

BERNIE   Yeah I'm just changing it a bit, giving it a bit more . . . you know . . . something extra . . .

BOB   Summat extra?

BERNIE   Yeah.

BOB   What like?

BERNIE   You know, make it a bit catchier.

BOB   Catchier?

BERNIE   Yeah, slicker, you know so it rhymes or something.

BOB   Let's have a look at the others . . . you know, for a laugh an' that. Give us it, Bernie . . . give us the paper . . .

BERNIE   For a laugh?

BOB   Yeah.

(BERNIE *reluctantly passes* BOB *the paper. Lights change.*)

RITA   Would you like to read one?

SILV   (*snaps*) No chance . . .

RITA   God you're horrible sometimes.

SILV   It's called self-preservation, Rita.

RITA   Maybe he just wants someone to believe in him.

SILV   You don't say.

RITA   Maybe he just wants to be loved.

SILV	By you?
RITA	Like you.
	(*Lights change.*)
BOB	So I'll help you, right . . . *you* mind, not me. Right?
SILV	Well if you want my help we start by binning this lot, right? (*The letters.*)
BOB	And we work it out. There's got to be a formula, see. A right way of wording these things to get the right response right?
SILV	I'll help you write a new one, 'cos whatever you put was giving off all the wrong signals. You've gotta sell yourself in the right way, right?
BERNIE RITA	Does it have to say that?
BOB SILV	'Course it does!
RITA	But why?
SILV	'Cos he has to read it and get an instant erection.
RITA	What, in the Daily Mail?
SILV	Eh?
RITA	The Daily Mail, will they allow it?
SILV	Ah well it's hidden, in't it? Ya know, between the lines. You say things like 'Tall leggy blonde likes fast cars and walks in the country'.
RITA	But I don't.
SILV	I know you don't but it's written in code ya see . . .
BERNIE	Why?
BOB	Why what?
BERNIE	Why is it in code?

BOB	Well it's obvious, in't it?
RITA	Is it?
BOB SILV	Course it is.
BOB	You have to keep 'em guessing see, not give the game away . . . get 'em curious, get 'em going . . . see what I'm saying?
RITA	But what does it mean?
SILV	It's understood only by that special someone on the same wavelength.
BOB	Someone feeling the same sexual vibes as you . . .
BERNIE	Is it?
SILV	Course it is. Ya see, 'Tall leggy blonde' means you're sexy.
BOB	'Fast cars' means you're very sexy . . .
SILV	And walks in the country means, well that you're very very very sexy . . .
RITA	So why can't you just say, 'I'm very sexy' . . .
BOB	S. E. X. That's what it's all about, see. Ya have to learn to write in code, say summat like 'Tall, dark and handsome, likes hot ladies who drive in the fast lane of life . . .'
BERNIE	And that keeps 'em guessing?
BOB	Exactly. You're halfway there, mate. You don't have to tell the whole truth . . .
SILV	Quick, I've got an idea.

(BOB *and* SILV *scribble.*)

BERNIE	I aren't tanned.
BOB	Not yet.

BERNIE	I go red and peel.
BOB	You can use fake.
RITA	I'm not a blonde.
SILV	Not yet.
RITA	But last time I dyed me hair it went green and fell out!
SILV	You can wear a wig.
BERNIE	But I ain't got a sports car.
BOB	You can say it's being serviced.
RITA	But I can't drive, I'm scared of traffic, even on me push bike I ride on the path.
BERNIE RITA	I can't speak Japanese!
SILV	It doesn't matter.
BOB	It's in code.
BOB SILV	And what does it mean?
BERNIE RITA	That I'm sexy?
BOB SILV	Exactly! Get 'em curious, get em going!
BOB	Hang on, no I've got it . . .
BERNIE	But I like this one.
BOB	No we need summat more, summat tells 'em what kind of bloke you're like inside . . . the inner you . . . the you that ain't come out yet . . .
SILV	The you yet to be discovered.
RITA	If you go over ten words it works out ever so expensive, Silv . . .

BOB	Right!
SILV	Finished!
BOB	It's perfect!
SILV	Quick, get it sent off!
BOB	Get things moving!
SILV	That'll knock 'em dead, kid!
BOB	It'll drive 'em wild, mate!
SILV	Fellas all over town rushing out and posting us letters . . . I mean you letters.
BOB	Hundreds of sex-starved women dying to meet us . . . meet you, mate . . .
SILV	You wait and see . . .
BOB	It's the start of something big.
SILV	I can feel it.
RITA	Can ya?
BOB	This is the new you, Bernie.
BERNIE	Is it?
SILV	The man of your dreams is out there Rita, waiting just for you.
BOB	She's out there Bernie . . . ready . . . all you have to do now mate, is . . .
RITA	Shit, it's nearly Valentine's Day . . .
SILV	Look, if God can make the world in six days, I'm sure he can find you a gorgeous bloke in ten!

(*Music. 'My Funny Valentine' plays as the lights fade to blackout.*)

ACT TWO

Bob *and* Bernie. Rita *and* Silv. *The two scenes merge as before.*

Bob   I don't understand it.

Bernie   I'm telling ya they've mucked the box numbers up again.

Bob   Three?

Silv   Oh my God!

Rita   How many?

Silv   Guess.

Rita   Ten?

Bob   Three?

Silv   Higher . . .

Rita   Fifteen?

Bob   Shit.

Rita   Bloody hell!

Bob   I don't understand it.

Bernie   It'll be the paper's fault.

Silv   It's amazin' . . .

Bob   Three?

Rita   More than twenty?

Silv   Yep . . .

Rita   Bloody hell!

Bernie   It's the box number again . . . they've mucked it up, Bob.

Silv   Come on, guess.

RITA Give us a clue.

BOB Three though . . . only three?

SILV Double it.

RITA Double what? Twenty? Shit!

BERNIE Plus being Bank Holiday, an' that . . .

RITA Forty?

SILV Add six.

RITA No?

BOB Three?

RITA Forty six?

SILV Yep!

BERNIE We should maybe give it a few more days.

RITA Forty six!

BERNIE You wait . . . there'll be loads.

BOB Yeah, I suppose so . . .

RITA God, where do we start?

BERNIE But we might as well check these ones out . . .

SILV Take your pick . . . (*She throws them into the air.*)

BERNIE (*holding up the three*) Which one do you want?

BOB You read 'em . . .

RITA Eenie Meenie Minie Mo . . .

BERNIE I'll open this one then . . . yeah?

RITA Catch a new man by his toe . . .

BERNIE Nice writing.

RITA	If he's a nutter let him go . . . Eenie Meenie Minie Mo . . . ! This one? Shall I read this one?
BERNIE	Just 'cos there's only three doesn't mean to say they're weirdos . . .
BOB	Just get on with it.
SILV	Wait! We can afford to be very choosy, right? So if his handwriting's disgusting, in red biro or he can't spell, mentions his mother, Sky television or collecting anything, we bin it — right?
RITA	Right . . .
BOB	Well?
SILV	What's he say?
BOB	Bernie . . . what's she say?
SILV	Rita? Come on . . . oh, give us it here . . . (*Reads.*) Bloody hell!
BOB	(*he has also taken the letter from* BERNIE) Jesus . . . she sounds alright . . .
BERNIE	Alright? She sounds bloody amazing!
SILV	He sounds . . . nice . . . too nice. There's gotta be a catch . . .
BOB	Mind you, notice she ain't sent a photo. I mean it's alright saying you're a model an' that but she could be lying . . .
SILV	He could be an expert, you know, at writing letters an' that.
RITA	He sounds great to me . . .
BERNIE	I like the sound of her . . .
SILV	But you've still got forty five others to read.
BOB	Read the other two . . . 'ere, I'll read one.
BERNIE	Well?

BOB	Hang on . . .
BERNIE	What's she like?
BOB	Alright . . . I think . . .
RITA	Well?
SILV	Sounds fine . . . ordinary but fine.
BOB	Nowt special but alright . . . this needs serious consideration though. We need to read all three. Study them. Paper quality, handwriting . . . content. We need to categorise them. Marks in order of . . . say, sex appeal . . . stuff like that, right? We can't rush into this . . . we've gotta work out the secret code . . . you know, what she's not sayin' an' that . . . right?
BERNIE	Can't we just meet them all?
SILV	We need to read every one. Put them in order. Best writing. Best envelopes . . . things like the fun factor . . . if they sound good looking or not, that sort of thing, right?
RITA	Yeah . . . God, forty six though. Blimey, what if they all sound as gorgeous as this one . . . 'ere, you'll have to help me get through 'em, Silv. We could hire city hall and line 'em all up . . . see who's the best snogger. Blimey, we ain't got long though . . .
SILV	What do ya mean?
RITA	Before Valentine's Day.
SILV	Oh shurrup and read them. (*Passes her a handful.*)
BOB	I expect we'll get loads tomorra. . .
BERNIE	We?
BOB	What?
BERNIE	You said "we".

BOB	Did I? I meant you. I reckon you'll probably get loads tomorra . . .

(BERNIE *steps forward, addressing the audience.*)

BERNIE	All over town swarms of lasses are reaching for pens and paper, paper of many colours . . . pink and lemon and baby blue, perfumed paper, personalised paper, paper pinched from work . . . all over town they're getting ready to write to . . .
BOB	Tall dark and handsome. Loves loving ladies with long legs. Tall blonde and handsome. Loves little ladies with loving legs? Tall bronzed God looking for same? Tall man seeks tall lady for cosy nights in.
BERNIE	Cuddly bloke with big personality seeks special lady to make feel ten feet tall . . .
RITA	Don't you think he sounds nice though?
SILV	What's the point of writing to an advert in the paper when you've got your own in? We've still got Don from Goole, John off Ings Road Estate, Fred the butcher and Frank "own business" to contact yet.
RITA	It's very honest though, in't it?
SILV	Too honest, there's probably a catch. Right. Plan of action . . . 'ave you got your watch, pen and note pad, change for telephone . . . your asthma pump? Good. Right . . . listen carefully 'cos if this is gonna work we have to keep to the rota, right? Rita? I said we have to stick to the rota, Rita, the rota, right?
RITA	I wonder how many replies he'd had . . .
SILV	Rita will you please concentrate? Right . . .
RITA	Here, I bet he's meeting someone tonight, an' all . . .

BERNIE	I feel a bit nervous Bob . . .
BOB	Trust me.
BERNIE	Maybe I should have just replied to one of the other adverts instead, I mean some sound real nice. Oh God . . . I feel a bit sick . . . shit, Bob. I think I'm coming down with summat . . . I feel all hot and shaky. Jesus Bob, look at that. (*Holding his hands out.*) I'll never hold a pint like that.
BOB	You'll be alright once you see her waiting, smiling an' that . . . dying to meet ya . . . excited an' that. You'll be great.

(*Lights change. Interior of two pubs.* RITA *and* BERNIE *are each sat with their dates, using two of the mannequins.*)

RITA	So . . .
BERNIE	Do you come here often?
RITA	I like it in here, don't you?
BERNIE	Yeah, nice lighting, tables, chairs an' that . . . nice.
RITA	Very nice . . . Cosy an' that . . .
BERNIE	Sort of old, well not old, I mean done up old fashioned, beams, carpets . . . pictures an' that . . . nice . . .
RITA	Them books look real . . . I mean I know they're real, I mean real old, dusty an' that.
BERNIE	You know in character with . . . everything else in here . . . old fashioned. Except you! God no, you're not old . . . actually I prefer summat a bit more modern than myself . . .
RITA	Sort of dead stylish with loads of metal and bright colours, you know, dead modern looking . . .

BERNIE	Neon lights.
RITA	Like a sort of bar really . . . you know, not a pub, a bar.
BERNIE	I like neon . . .
RITA	A sort of cocktail bar.
BERNIE	You know, neon lights . . . not the ones that flash on and off . . . just the . . . ones that keep still . . . the stylish ones. American looking.
RITA	I love cocktails . . .
BERNIE	Like in America.
RITA	I had one once called . . . oh 'eck, it sounds a bit mucky.
BERNIE	Neon . . . lights . . . nice word that in't it? Neon lights.
RITA	A long slow screwdriver . . . summat like that. So . . .
BERNIE	So . . . do you, you know . . .
RITA	Come in 'ere often?

(*Lights change.*)

BERNIE	Bob, you've gotta help me out!
RITA	I've got to have some help, Silv. I can't see this many blokes in one week, it'll kill me. Will you help me . . . please?
SILV	Right . . . check your watch . . . half six to nine you see the dentist. Nine to ten thirty you see the builder, bank clerk and unemployed computer operator from Brid'. And that mature travel agent from Beverley. Right?
BERNIE	I can't keep this up, will you meet them, an' all?
BOB	We got the librarian, and Donna the belly dancer from Doncaster yet. I'll give you the nod, you

BERNIE	Oh right . . .
BOB	Give 'em exactly seventy five minutes each. You've set your alarm, right?
BERNIE	Right. (*He checks for breath freshener and asthma pump.*)
SILV	Don't forget the get-out clauses, right? Sick dog at home, asthma attack, flashing lights?
RITA	Migraine . . . strict father . . . er . . . allergy to his after shave, fear of enclosed spaces . . .
SILV	Good. Don't kiss, give phone numbers, addresses, second names or correct age. Don't tell him where you work and strictly under no circumstances make any promises.
RITA	Right . . . Oooh, God, what if I get it wrong?
SILV	Final get-out clause.
RITA	Go to bog and leg it . . .
BOB	In case of emergencies?
BERNIE	Spill drink?
BOB	Then?
BERNIE	Lose contact lens, crawl out the door and leg it!

(*Lights change.* BERNIE *and* RITA *with blind dates number two.*)

RITA	No I don't drink much as a rule . . . you did? You was? (*She laughs, nervously.*) Yeah . . . I always thought the AA was them road people.
BERNIE	So do you fancy summat to eat? No . . . I hate being sick an' all . . . But you do eat now, though? No? Oh well, we can just drink . . .

RITA	So you're cured now then?
BERNIE	Foods not up to much in 'ere, anyway . . .
RITA	So do you always drink straight orange squash or do you like other soft drinks?
BERNIE	I had a virus once, didn't eat for nearly four days . . .
RITA	Actually I like St Clements . . .
BERNIE	Now you come to mention it I was sick a bit an' all . . .
RITA	(*sings*) Oranges and lemons say the bells of St Clements . . .
BERNIE	I had the shits terrible — I mean the runs terrible.
RITA	It's fresh orange, like Britvic or summat, and lemonade. Together in one glass . . . with ice . . . it's nice.
BERNIE	I'm alright now, though. Blimey, I 'ad a massive tea . . . stew and dumplings . . . me mam's dumplings are smashing . . . I always 'ave two. Right big 'uns, an' all . . . smashing they are.
RITA	So do you sometimes still get the urge, you know, to have summat stronger?
BERNIE	Do I think you're fat? No . . . blimey, no. I mean it's hard to tell, you know, with your coat on an' that, but no . . . I was just thinking to meself actually . . . you know, how . . . thin . . . I mean slim you looked . . . would you like another glass of water? They 'ave that fizzy water in 'ere, you know . . .
RITA	Actually I once thought I had a drink problem one Christmas. I don't know whether it was because I was depressed or what but all I seemed to do is drink.

ACT TWO

BERNIE   Are you alright? Do you want a hanky?

RITA   You name it, I drank it. Snowballs, sherry, cherry brandy, port and lemon, Bailey's, God I was never sober . . .

BERNIE   Don't cry . . . look, do you want summat stronger to drink? A brandy or summat? Don't cry.

RITA   Blimey, I was practically an alcoh — You alright? Your hand's shaking a bit. Eh? Well, I ain't finished this yet, but sod it, I'll have a Bacardi and Coke with ice, ta . . .

BERNIE   Did I say something to upset you?

RITA   'Ere, I thought you didn't drink no more?

(*Lights change.*)

BERNIE   One more each, what do ya reckon? For luck.

BOB   You've gotta be kidding!

RITA   But this time let's get in touch with one out of the paper.

BERNIE   Put a daft one in from us both, like a double date or summat.

RITA   They'll be loads in tonight 'cos it's nearly Valentine's Day!

BERNIE   Get it in the paper tonight . . . replies in time for Valentine's Day!

SILV   You are joking, right?

RITA   Go on, one last try . . . for luck.

BERNIE   Pick say, the first letter we get, first through the door, first on the mat, eh?

BOB   And go through all this again?

BERNIE   No this time it'll be a laugh 'cos we'll do a double one, summat daft.

RITA Go on, we might as well. Let's put our faith in fate, eh?

(*Music plays, the theme from The Good, the Bad and the Ugly.* RITA *reads the ad.*)

BUTCH CASSIDY AND THE SUNDANCE KID. LOOKING FOR THE RIGHT GALS TO RIDE INTO THE SUNSET WITH.

BERNIE (*reading the reply letter*) "Dear Butch and the Kid, Pistols at the ready guys, cause Calamity Jane and Annie Oakley are coming to town — ready for a showdown at 'Lucky's Diner', Paragon Street, 8:00 PM, VALENTINE'S DAY!"

(*Lights change. Music continues as* BOB *and* BERNIE *put on cowboy hats, holsters and guns, and saunter down to the front of the stage to the bar at Lucky's Diner.* BOB *is enjoying himself immensely, but* BERNIE *remains tentative. The music gradually fades out.*)

BOB Drink your rye, kid . . .

BERNIE Eh?

BOB Your whiskey . . . drink it . . . (BOB *downs his in one.*)

BERNIE I don't really like whiskey, Bob.

BOB 'Ere shove that in your gob. (BOB *passes him a cigar.*)

BERNIE No . . . it'll set me chest off.

BOB For God's sake, just try and look cool, Bernie. (*Pause.*) What time is it? (*He spits.*)

BERNIE I dunno . . . Bob, the landlady keeps looking over here. I don't think she likes you spitting on the carpet.

BOB Tough!

BERNIE	She'll chuck us out.
BOB	(*putting his gun on the table*) I don't think so, kid . . .
BERNIE	These boots are bloody killing me!
BOB	Bernie, are you gonna moan all night or are you gonna act more like a cowboy?
BERNIE	It's just that I feel a bit daft, that's all, and this hat's making me head itch.

(BOB *picks up his gun and uses it to knock* BERNIE'S *hat off his head.*)

BOB	Alright? So give over moanin' . . . drink your whiskey.
BERNIE	It makes me gag.
BOB	Down it in one . . .
BERNIE	(*he does*) Ugh . . .
BOB	Keep your eye on the door . . .
BERNIE	What time do these costumes have to be back tomorrow?
BOB	Bernie, just keep an eye on the door, alright?
BERNIE	I think I've been ripped off, though . . . I'm sure this waistcoat's a woman's.
BOB	Will you shurrup moaning.
BERNIE	I know, well I'm just a bit nervous . . . people are walking in now, Bob.
BOB	Chicks?
BERNIE	Yeah . . .
BOB	Dressed like cowgirls?
BERNIE	Yeah.

BOB	They looking over 'ere, or what?
BERNIE	No . . .
BOB	No? Are you sure?
BERNIE	No. Shit, Bob. There's loads of 'em all dressed the same . . . oh, shit . . . they're all dressed like cowgirls . . . and cowboys . . . oh 'eck.
BOB	What?
BERNIE	I think it's a theme pub, Bob.
BOB	Oh brilliant. Fucking brilliant!
BERNIE	How was I to know? It was their choice.
BOB	Exactly, they're taking the piss!
BERNIE	They might recognise us . . .
BOB	How? Or have you brought badges?

(*Lights change.* RITA *and* SILV, *outside, dressed as cowgirls.*)

SILV	Rita, will you 'urry up, we're already late!
RITA	Oh God these bleedin' boots are agony!
SILV	Right. Listen. Seeing as it was your bright idea to drag me 'ere in the first place I'll decide which one I like best and you take the other one, right?
RITA	Suppose so . . .
SILV	Well take your coat off then.
RITA	Oh God, do I have to?
SILV	'Course you do! Else they won't recognise us will they?
RITA	Shit.
SILV	And take your glasses off an' all.

RITA   But I won't be able to see owt . . .

SILV   Right! Here we go . . . get your guns out guys, Annie's back in town . . .

RITA   I thought I was Annie?

SILV   You're Calamity Jane, so shurrup moanin' and get your gun out . . . Rita, where's your gun?

RITA   It's in me coat pocket. I feel daft . . .

SILV   Take your coat off, get your gun out and for God's sake try and look attractive . . .

RITA   Oh shit.

(They both walk through the saloon doors.)

SILV   I don't believe it!

RITA   What?

SILV   This is bloody typical, this is!

RITA   *(putting her glasses on)* Everybody's dressed like cowboys!

SILV   Brilliant . . . just brilliant.

RITA   And cowgirls.

SILV   You don't say . . .

RITA   Oh shit!

SILV   They'll think we're taking the piss!

RITA   Just think, Silv. Out there amongst all them cowboys, there's two just waiting for us.

SILV   Oh God . . .

BOB   This is a bloody joke.

BERNIE   Every woman reckons she's Annie Oakley or Calamity bloody Jane.

BOB   I'm well aware of that THANKS MATE.

BERNIE	So what shall we do now?
BOB	Get pissed.
RITA	God I've never seen so many cowboys in me life. Don't they look realistic though . . .
SILV	Oh aye, until they open their gobs and they're off Ings Road Estate.
RITA	They take it ever so seriously though, don't they? That bloke over there showed me his guns . . . they're ever so real-looking.
SILV	Really? Ask him if I can borrow one, will ya?
BERNIE	Bob, there's a bloke in the bog reckons he's Buffalo Bill . . . well, on a weekend anyway. He's a bus driver really. It's great, in't it? Have you noticed Bob, they don't say hiya, they all say "howdy, partner" . . . HOWDY PARTNER!
BOB	Bernie, do you ever get the feeling that you're jinxed?
BERNIE	Me?
BOB	Yes you.
BERNIE	Why me?
BOB	'Cos this was your fucking bright idea.
BERNIE	So?
BOB	AND look at us both, stood 'ere like a couple of cowboys . . . Jesus, I must have been off my head to listen to you . . .
BERNIE	Maybe you're the one who's jinxed.
RITA	'Ere . . . don't he look like Clint Eastwood?
SILV	No.
RITA	You're not even looking.

ACT TWO

SILV I don't have to, you're blind as a bat without your glasses on . . . are you gonna go to the bar?

RITA I went last time.

SILV Look, it's your fault I'm 'ere so get to the bar.

RITA Well, if that Wild Bill Hitchcock grabs my arse again I'm gonna smack 'im one . . .

SILV I'll have a double.

BOB Make it a double.

RITA You'll get pissed.

SILV That's the intention.

BERNIE Whiskey?

BOB Yeah . . .

BERNIE God, you're gonna be off your head.

BOB Good.

SILV Rita, you'd better put your glasses on . . .

(RITA *and* BERNIE *bump into each other.*)

RITA Oh sorry.

BERNIE No it was . . . my fault . . .

(*Music starts to play in the background.*)

BERNIE Rita?

RITA Bernie?

BERNIE Rita . . .

RITA Bernie . . .

BERNIE God!

RITA I can't believe it!

BERNIE Shit.

RITA	Bernie!
BERNIE	Rita!
RITA	God!
BERNIE	Shit!
RITA	It's you.
BERNIE	I can't believe it!
RITA	Me neither . . . blimey! You're a cowboy.
BERNIE	Yeah . . . no, well only for tonight. I'm a window cleaner really.
RITA	That's nice.

(*Pause.*)

BERNIE	Are you Annie?
RITA	No . . . I'm Calamity Jane . . . but I've got a gun . . .
BERNIE	'Ave ya?
RITA	Yeah, it's in me coat pocket. Shit . . . are you Butch?
BOB	No I'm The Kid . . . Bob's Butch.
RITA	Bob?
BERNIE	Yeah . . . he's sat over there . . . well he was. He's pissed off . . . he doesn't really like being a cowboy.
RITA	Silv's here an' all . . . she's Annie . . . well, for tonight anyway . . . mind you, so are half the lasses in 'ere . . . it suits ya.
BERNIE	What?
RITA	Being a cowboy . . .
BERNIE	Does it?
RITA	Yeah.

BERNIE	You look different.
RITA	Fatter?
BERNIE	Nice.
RITA	So you're a window cleaner?
BERNIE	Yeah. I own me own round . . .
RITA	I knew you'd be a businessman one day.
BERNIE	I can't believe it's you!
RITA	I know . . . I shock meself sometimes.
BERNIE	I've moved.
RITA	I know. I noticed.
BERNIE	Did ya?
RITA	Yeah . . . specially when they pulled your old house down.
BERNIE	Eh? Oh, joke, right? (*He laughs.*)
RITA	Shit, it's Valentine's Day . . . night.
BERNIE	I know . . .
RITA	Twenty years tonight.
BERNIE	I've thought about you.
RITA	Was I fat?
BERNIE	Eh?
RITA	When you thought about me?
BERNIE	No, naked. Joke . . . (*Music — Crazy, by Patsy Cline.*) You was lovely, like now . . . do you want to dance?
RITA	Only if you've kept practising . . .
BERNIE	I've got a full-length one now . . .

RITA	I know, I can feel it . . .
BERNIE	I think that's me gun . . .
RITA	Is it loaded?
BERNIE	I like you Rita . . .
RITA	I know . . . are you sure this is your gun?

(*The music swells as they dance back into the present.*)

BERNIE	This suit is gonna be great . . . I can feel it. It feels right, do you know what I mean Bob? Hey, this suit was made for me. Want it, Bob? Cool suit, eh Bob?
BOB	The suit's shit, Bernie.
BERNIE	Joke, right?
BOB	. . . Joke.
BERNIE	God I can feel it Bob.
BOB	Well take your hands out of your pockets and sit down.
BERNIE	No I can . . . I can really feel it . . .
BOB	What?
BERNIE	Life.
SILV	I think you should wear it up, with bits dangling down, tonged into ringlets and the back sort of scooped into a forties roll . . . maybe a bit of a wispy fringe to soften it and some pearl earrings and a delicate baby pearl necklace . . .
RITA	Pearls mean tears. There's been enough tears already.
SILV	What you wearing then?
RITA	Me little golden heart.

SILV	I thought it got broke.
RITA	It did but I'm having it mended.
BERNIE	I can't believe it. I've always hated western films. I preferred war films. You always liked westerns, didn't you Bob?
BOB	Aye, when I was about six.
RITA	Bernie's having his suit made-to-measure.
SILV	Aye, well he'll have to won't he?
RITA	What do you mean?
SILV	'Cos his mam said so . . .
RITA	ACTUALLY IT WAS MY IDEA.
SILV	The first of many, eh?
RITA	What do you mean?
SILV	Changing him . . .
RITA	I don't want to change him.
SILV	'Course you don't.
RITA	I like him the way he is . . . I allus did.
SILV	So what's it gonna be?
RITA	I've told you, made-to-measure, by a master tailor.
SILV	With a matching cowboy hat?
RITA	Funny.
SILV	You're tellin' me . . .
RITA	What's that mean?
SILV	You met him in a bloody theme pub!
RITA	So . . .

SILV	A GROWN MAN DRESSED AS A FRIGGIN' COWBOY!
RITA	You've never liked him, 'ave you?
SILV	It was a joke.

(*Lights change. A factory whistle blows. Back in time.*)

BERNIE	Rita, I've come to see you.
RITA	I can see . . . wish I'd known, I'd have had me hair set. (*Laughs. A pause.*) Is everything alright?
BERNIE	Yeah . . . No. I can't see you no more.
RITA	But you can hear me still?
BERNIE	I still live with me mam.
RITA	You're lucky. I still live with me mam and dad . . . three budgies and a fat old dog called Fanny.
BERNIE	Fanny?
RITA	Different generation.
BERNIE	You make me laugh . . .
RITA	It's the way I tell 'em . . . or maybe I'm just daft . . .
BERNIE	No you . . . I don't really do this you see . . .
RITA	What? Hang around factory gates?
BERNIE	See women more than once.
RITA	Playboy, eh?
BERNIE	It's not something I do . . .
RITA	No, you just go on blind dates with Bob dressed as cowboys.
BERNIE	Yes. No! I suppose so. I like you Rita, I do . . .

RITA	But not enough though, eh?
BERNIE	I don't know how to talk to you like this.
RITA	No, well it's probably because you've got a bad memory.
BERNIE	What do ya mean?
RITA	You've forgotten what Bob told you to say.
BERNIE	I'm sorry?
RITA	You look it, but than again you always did.
BERNIE	What do you mean?
RITA	Sorry for yourself. Hard done by. It comes from living under someone's shadow, Bernie. It's cold isn't it?
BERNIE	I don't know what you want me to say . . .
RITA	You've said it . . . you can go now. Maybe see you in another twenty years, eh?
BERNIE	The blind dates were a mistake. I wasn't really looking for someone. I was just seeing if I could do it.
RITA	What, to impress Bob?
BERNIE	No. Myself.
RITA	And did you?
BERNIE	No.
RITA	Shame.
BERNIE	I wasn't really looking for someone . . . not really. You was though, weren't you?
RITA	Yep.
BERNIE	And will you look again?
RITA	Yep.

BERNIE	I hope you find someone . . .
RITA	I'll stay away from cowboys though. They're all the same, ride into town, break your heart. Ride back out again. Me mother did warn me. Never trust a man with a loaded gun . . .
BERNIE	I'm a window cleaner.
RITA	By day . . . "The Kid" by night.
BERNIE	I clean windows.
RITA	That makes sense . . .
BERNIE	I have a van.
RITA	I have a bus pass.
BERNIE	I like you Rita.
RITA	The bus pass impressed you, eh?
BERNIE	I don't know how to do this . . .
RITA	Do what? Say you like me?
BERNIE	I feel daft.
RITA	(*kisses him*) So do I . . . feel . . . (*She takes his hands and puts them inside her coat.*) Feel . . .
BERNIE	Shit, Rita!
RITA	Don't crush 'em!
BERNIE	They're rock hard . . .
RITA	They're frozen.
BERNIE	I better stop, I might melt them.
RITA	I don't mind.
BERNIE	Couldn't you lose your job?
RITA	No. People do it all the time . . .
BERNIE	I do like you.

RITA	I know.
BERNIE	It's just that I can't stop thinking about —
RITA	(*kisses him*) Bernie. (*She kisses him again.*) Shut up . . .
BERNIE	Your peas are melting, Rita.
RITA	Sod the peas, feel these!
BERNIE	Oh shit . . .
RITA	Bernie . . .

(*They are kissing more frantically now. The theme from Brief Encounter plays.*)

BERNIE	Rita . . .
RITA	Bernie . . .
BERNIE	Oh shit, your peas have leaked.
RITA	No wonder.
BERNIE	You're getting wet.
RITA	I know.
BERNIE	Oh God . . .
RITA	You can take a bag home for your mam.
BERNIE	Rita . . .
RITA	I can get 'er sweet corn an' all.
BERNIE	I like you Rita . . .
RITA	Proppa on the cob an' that . . . not just bits.
BERNIE	Good, 'cause I hate peas . . . do you still like me?
RITA	What about sweet corn?
BERNIE	What about me?
RITA	Yes . . . I like you Bernie.

BERNIE	Yes I like sweet corn . . . and you. I like you an' all, Rita . . .
RITA	Do ya?
BERNIE	Yeah.
RITA	Good.
BERNIE	I always did.
RITA	I know . . . Bernie.
BERNIE	What?
RITA	I can get fish cakes an' all.
BERNIE	I love you Rita.
RITA	Proppa cod an' that, not just fish guts . . .
BERNIE	I'm allergic to fish. Will you marry me?
RITA	So am I . . .
BERNIE	When I said I wasn't really looking for someone I meant it, I wasn't. Because I only ever wanted you.
RITA	Oh 'eck, me peas 'ave gone all mushy . . .

(*Lights change. The present day.*)

RITA	Shit, what's eating you, Silv? I love him. I love him a lot . . . I allus did.
SILV	He moved away Rita, never even said goodbye.
RITA	Who we talking about here, Bernie . . . or Bob?
SILV	This place is freezing . . . is it raining again?
RITA	Why can't you be happy for me?
SILV	I am . . . but what was the point in going to all that trouble of meeting all them other fellas if you're gonna settle for some idiot you knew years ago.

RITA	He's not an idiot.
SILV	He's a bloody window cleaner, for God's sake.
RITA	And we pack peas . . . so? What does that make us?
SILV	How do you know he really cares?
RITA	I do . . . that's all.
BERNIE	Well this is it mate. I'm nearly there. I can't believe it. Me and Rita . . . every night together. Bloody hell, can you imagine it?
BOB	I'd rather not, ta . . .
BERNIE	Every night in the same bed as a woman.
BOB	No, with Rita. Joke.
BERNIE	Every night . . . God it's like a miracle in't it? It's like everything you've ever wanted for Christmas, it's like winning summat, in't it?
BOB	Er . . . no.
RITA	Oh Silv, will I really look alright in this dress?
SILV	Yes.
RITA	Do you really think so?
SILV	Yes . . .
RITA	Be happy for me, Silv . . .
SILV	I am. God what do you want me to do, write it in blood?
BERNIE	Bloody hell! A whole hundred percent total female body in bed with me every night . . . flesh against flesh . . .
BOB	I think I need some air . . .
BERNIE	Sex on tap. Sex on demand. Shit, sex every day for the rest of my life . . .

Bob	I think you need some air . . .
Bernie	Sex around the clock.
Bob	Until she comes home one night in a mood. Then it's the settee for you, mate. This place gives me the creeps. These things have been watching you, Bernie — and thinking . . . flesh against flesh? Poor cow. Thank God we're made of plastic . . .
Rita	(*looking at herself*) I should have gone for a darker white . . .
Silv	What, like grey?
Rita	No, a sort of off-white . . . summat less . . . white.
Silv	What about black?
Rita	Funny.
Silv	What about red then?
Rita	Eh?
Silv	Dress.
Rita	Red?
Silv	Some do.
Rita	Not me.
Silv	Stick with white then.
Rita	You'd suit red.
Silv	White's alright.
Rita	Mind you, you'd suit black an' all.
Silv	White's just white.
Rita	Black veil, black dress.
Silv	It's feminine is white, fattening but feminine.

RITA	Black fucking eye. Joke.
BERNIE	Me mother's been doin' a lot of crying recently . . .
BOB	What do ya mean recently, she's been crying all her life.
BERNIE	This is different.
BOB	Women are always crying, Bernie. They like it.
BERNIE	No this is proppa crying, it's not in front of people. It's on her own in her room. No, now she only cries when she thinks no one can hear her.
BOB	'Ere do you think I should grow a tash, like what's-his-name in Gone with the Wind?
BERNIE	She cries at that an' all. But that's a big sort of cry. The crying coming from her room is a sort of whimper, like a puppy.
BOB	Bernie, I'm asking you an important question.
BERNIE	Why?
BOB	'Cos I think a tash'll suit me.
BERNIE	So why does she do it in her room?
BOB	Do ya know I reckon it might only take me two, maybe three days, just a thin 'un. I think it'll look good, refined an' that . . .
BERNIE	I've heard her cry like this before though, when I was little and me gran died . . .
BOB	How long would it take you?
BERNIE	What?
BOB	. . . To grow a tash?
BERNIE	Dunno. I don't think it would join up in the middle 'cos I had chicken pox bad as a kid. I wonder if Rita cries at films?
BOB	Or maybe a beard?

BERNIE	I admire that in a woman.
BOB	A beard?
BERNIE	No it'd take to long.
RITA	Me bloody hair's all over!
SILV	All over where?
RITA	My head.
SILV	(*sarcastic*) No . . .
RITA	A MESS.
SILV	Needs sortin', that's all.
RITA	True.
SILV	Like your face.
RITA	True. Joke. My face? Funny. Oh, why do hairstyles always grow out?
SILV	'Cos we're alive.
RITA	Grow into a mess.
SILV	It's one of life's great mysteries, Rita.
RITA	Twenty-odd quid. Nice hair-do. Great. Six weeks later, bloody mop. Mess.
SILV	There's no fooling you, eh?
RITA	Hairdressers have got it made.
SILV	Oh, sit down . . .
RITA	Mind you, Bernie allus likes my hair. Mess or no mess he allus says, "your hair looks nice, Rita". That must mean summat.
SILV	Aye Rita, it does. It means he dun't look at you properly.
BERNIE	I think Rita'd make a good mother.

BOB	'Ere, what film is this then, Bernie . . .
BERNIE	Dumbo?
BOB	Funny. Here's a clue . . . "May 10th, 1972. Thank God for all the rain which has helped wash the garbage and the trash off the sidewalks . . ."
BERNIE	I'm a lucky man.
BOB	Taxi Driver.
BERNIE	I am. I know it. I'm a very lucky man . . .
BOB	That's a matter of opinion. Mate. (*He does his Robert De Niro impression, very aggressive.*) You talking to me? Eh? Eh? You talking to me?
BERNIE	What do ya mean?
BOB	Eh?
BERNIE	You said that's a matter of opinion. What do you mean?
BOB	I was talking about De Nero . . . farting around . . . doing bits from films. It used to make you laugh once, remember?
BERNIE	No.
BOB	(*building up, with a mean edge*) Things getting on top of you are they?
BERNIE	NO.
BOB	Things starting to build up inside ya, are they?
BERNIE	It's this room . . .
BOB	Is it?
RITA	What do you mean?
SILV	'Bout what?
RITA	Bernie not looking at me? What's that mean?

SILV	It was a joke.
RITA	A joke.
SILV	Yes, a joke.
RITA	Or maybe I'm the real joke, eh?
SILV	Rita, I was having a laugh.
RITA	At me.
SILV	With you. But obviously now you're almost somebody's wife you've lost your sense of humour.
RITA	Or maybe it's Bernie you think's the joke.
SILV	Yes you are a joke. Yes Bernie is a joke . . . is that what you wanted? Satisfied now?
RITA	You're jealous!
SILV	Of two jokes?
RITA	This is his fault . . .
SILV	Oh shurrup Rita . . .
RITA	See the way you said 'somebody's wife'. I'm not just somebody's wife, I'm Bernie's.
SILV	Not yet you're not.
RITA	You just can't stand to see me happy . . . just because you're incapable of loving someone doesn't mean to say I am. You're not incapable, you're just scared. Why Silv . . . ask yourself why?
BERNIE	What did you mean?
BOB	You talkin' to me? Eh? Eh? You talkin' to me?
BERNIE	I said I was a lucky man. You said that is a matter of opinion. What the fuck did you mean?
BOB	You talkin' to me? Eh? Eh? You talkin' to me?

BERNIE Yes.

BOB Yes?

BERNIE YES!

BOB Look Bernie, them other lasses, right? We've still got their phone numbers, right? Why don't we give a couple of 'em a ring tonight, eh? Go on a double date? It'll be a laugh. Get you laid man!

BERNIE No.

BOB It'll be a laugh.

BERNIE I said NO! I love Rita.

BOB Right then . . . fine. Great. Fan-fucking-tastic mate.

BERNIE I've always loved Rita. You used to like Silv. I know you did. Why don't you sort it out? Whatever happened that night, well . . . it was a long time ago. The past . . . you can't change the past . . . but you can accept it.

SILV Was all like a dream. Head was spinning. Was all like a dream. Not nice. Not bad. Not real. Dress was up. Hands. Legs. Mouth . . . Tongue was everywhere. Grabbing and biting and sucking and kissing . . . we never kissed . . . why?

BOB I wanted to be summat. Carry it. Walk with it. Be summat bigger. I wanted to take what I wanted. Grab it, and if I felt like it . . . yeah, I wanted to squash it. Why not? Why the fuck not? Tell me that, eh? You just tell me . . . NO I DON'T GIVE A SHIT. RIGHT? RIGHT? NO SIR. GERMANY. ARMY. UNIFORM. SOLDIER. SIR? YES SIR!

RITA You was both just kids. You didn't know what you was doing. Silv, meet him . . . work it out. Forgive him. Forgive each other. You used to think a lot about him once, I know you did . . . and he did you. You was both daft, that's all.

SILV	Was easy. First a bit of smoke and then a flame. Was easy.
BERNIE	You didn't know how to show someone you liked 'em. Give her another chance . . . give yourself another chance . . .
BOB	I can't. So drop it, right?
BERNIE	So nothing's changed.
BOB	No.
SILV	Then bench and back wall. It took no time. Was easy. Beautiful. Run, he said. We've gotta run . . . but I didn't.
BERNIE	You still can't do it, can you? Can't back down. Show that side of you that's human. That side of you that wants something real. Wants to be like everyone else and be loved. There's no shame in it Bob. Loving someone is not being weak. It's being honest. It's what life is about.
BOB	Oh I'll get me fuckin' violin out in a minute, shall I?
BERNIE	See what I mean, your impossible to reach.
BOB	Reach?
BERNIE	Yeah . . .
BOB	(*moving closer*) Here, is that close enough for ya? Well go on then, reach me . . . go on. What is it you wanna reach, eh? Me heart? (*He rips open his shirt.*) Well go on then, you know where it is, you're the fuckin' expert on hearts all of a sudden . . . rip me open and grab it . . . (*He pulls out a pen knife.*) Pull it out and have a fucking good look at it!
BERNIE	Bob . . .
BOB	Come on Bernie, you do wanna see if I've got one, don't yer? Eh? I can tell you what we could do, we could cut yours out an' all, and compare

... see whose is biggest, eh? I'm being passionate ... like you. Have you got any other brilliant fuckin' words of wisdom for me? What else am I incapable of doing, eh? Maybe I'm incapable of a lot more ... like maybe being a man. Eh? And staying in the army? Well, what do you think?

BERNIE I never said that.

BOB You didn't have to ... (*He starts to cut his hand open.*)

SILV I couldn't move ... like I was rooted to the ground or summat ... I couldn't run ... I can't, I said. You go ... He held his hand out for me but I just stood there staring into the flames.

BERNIE Don't do that ... Bob, what are you doing that for?

BOB Pain.

BERNIE Pain?

BOB That's what being a man's all about, in't it?

BERNIE Bob, don't do that ...

BOB What a man, eh?

BERNIE You're upset, that's all ...

BOB Upset?

BERNIE You've been in here too long. You need some fresh air.

BOB Air?

SILV The air was full of black smoke, I couldn't breathe. Me cheeks were burning. Bob had on his white suit. He looked like a god ... I did it for you, I said. You're nearly a soldier. Suddenly he just hit me. Hard, in my face. I didn't even flinch. What you done that for? What did he do that for?

BOB	How much you can take in and how much you can give.
SILV	Then the cops came. Fire engines. All I kept thinking was, I love you, soldier . . .
BOB	Pain. Right? Yes Sir . . . 'Cos you are a soldier aren't you, Chapman? Yes Sir . . . What's wrong with you then, Chapman? Are you scared, Chapman? Do you want your mother? No Sir. I can't hear you Chapman. NO SIR! I still can't hear you. NO SIR!
SILV	He was crying in the police station. Who did it, love? Me, I said. He says it was him. Who did it, love? Me, I said. Why? Because I was cold. Why? Because I was cold. Did he hit you? No. I did it, it was nowt to do with him, he's nearly a soldier. Why did you do it? Because I was scared . . . because he was leaving me . . .
BOB	How much you can take . . . and how much you can give . . .
SILV	Did he hit you? YES. HE DID IT BECAUSE I WOULDN'T DO IT WITH HIM. BECAUSE I WOULDN'T LET HIM. HE SMACKED ME IN THE FACE AND SET FIRE TO THE SHELTER. HE DID IT. IT WAS HIM.
BERNIE	Bob? Are you alright?
BOB	I can't . . . do it no more Sir . . . PAIN. Blood brothers? Joke. Are you cold?
BERNIE	No.
BOB	Did you hear that noise?
BERNIE	No . . . you alright, Bob?
BOB	It's alright, it's just cats . . .
BERNIE	Do you want summat for your cut? Bob?

Bob	They sound like babies crying for their mams . . .
Bernie	Bob, I didn't mean to have a go at you . . .
Bob	It's just cats havin' it off . . . that's all.
Bernie	I can't hear anything.

(*The lights change.* Bob *and* Silv *in the past.*)

Bob	She came to look for me. I knew she would. Who could resist that suit, right? She was cold. I could tell. Nervous a bit. She'd been drinking. I could smell it . . . sweet cider. Too sweet.
Silv	Don't laugh at me . . . I said don't laugh at me! Stop it . . . but he didn't . . .
Bob	I don't know what happened . . . one minute it was great . . . the next it was different. Her face changed. I was laughing and her face changed.
Silv	All I kept thinking was, don't cry. Don't let him see you cry . . .
Bob	She sort of stared right through me . . . like I was summat bad.
Silv	Why? I don't like kissing . . .
Bob	Never did, couldn't explain . . . never did. I wanted to tell her but all I could do was . . . me mam used to slobber all over me old man. Even when he needed a shave, fag in his gob . . . stinking fuckin' beer breath . . . she'd be all over him. Ear. Neck . . . all over him . . .
Silv	No don't cry . . . laugh, don't cry . . .
Bob	She once hung onto his legs and he just dragged her across the room, like a dog, like a dog with a fuckin' bone that won't let go . . . half laughing, half crying . . . her skirt pulled up to her waist. I could see her thighs . . . red and bruised.

SILV	Then the lip wobbles. Then I shake. Then I can't stop . . .
BOB	I don't kiss . . .
SILV	Not just a little cry, a big cry. A shaking cry . . . me eyes screwed up and me mouth all twisted . . . DON'T TOUCH ME!
BOB	Don't cry like that . . .
SILV	DON'T LOOK AT ME! DON'T LOOK AT ME . . . and he didn't, he just stood there . . . calm. I could hear some cats and the trains . . . where do all those trains take people? I mean really . . . where do they go? Don't look at me . . .
BOB	I won't. Just stop crying . . .
SILV	He was so quiet. Unmoved . . . and I just stopped. Me eyes . . . me face . . . I just stopped . . .
BOB	She had mascara all over her face.
SILV	I laid down on the bench and pulled me skirt up over me thighs. I knew me face was ugly from crying . . . I felt lucky to have him. I could feel his hand . . . his breath . . . his weight . . . I felt lucky to have him on top of me . . . still wanting me . . .
BOB	She wanted me to do it . . .
SILV	I was willing him to. I was biting me lip to stop myself from crying and willing him to . . . no kissing . . . listen I said, it's them cats again . . . dirty buggers . . . listen I said, it's that train . . . you'll be on one tomorrow . . .
BOB	I wanted to frighten her . . . take her hard . . . I wanted to be heavy and hard on top . . . I could feel her shaking . . .
SILV	He tried to put it in me but he couldn't. I could feel him fumbling but he couldn't do it . . . and I knew it wouldn't work . . . nothing was ever

gonna be the same. I'd spoilt it, see . . . because I cried. Cried because I wanted him . . . and laughed because I cried . . .

(*The lights change.*)

BOB Women are allus crying, Bernie.

SILV It was my fault, I did it . . .

BERNIE I know you care about her Bob . . . you should tell her. Everyone deserves a second chance.

BOB Maybe someone else had mine . . . I know why . . . I should have done something to help her. I know it . . . I've allus known it.

RITA You should tell him about the baby, he should know, Silv. No one'd blame you, you was dead young . . .

SILV It was nowt to do with him. (*Pause.*) You're gonna look nice . . . smashing. You're gonna look lovely . . .

RITA Do you think so?

SILV I keep thinking about all them letters.

RITA Forty six . . .

SILV They weren't all losers, not really. They weren't all sad cases living with their mothers . . .

RITA Not all. Just some, the nice ones.

SILV That's where we're different, see. You like . . .

(*A beat.*)

RITA Sad cases who live with their mams?

SILV I never said that.

RITA And what do you like Silv? Bastards? Liars? Con artists . . . fellas that shit all over people? Lie to their best mates and fuck people's lives up? Eh? Is that the sort of bloke you prefer?

SILV	Shouldn't you be taking that dress off now, you know how you sweat . . . 'ere, I'll help you.
RITA	I don't want your help!
SILV	What's that mean?
RITA	You work it out . . .
BERNIE	Bob, do you think I'm too soft for a bloke?
BOB	I've never admitted this to meself before Bernie, but De Nero is not a tall bloke. You just think he is 'cos he's so fucking cool. (*Pause.*) I know what your problem is mate . . . the fear of the unknown. Rita isn't gonna laugh at ya, ya know . . . she loves ya, Bernie.
BERNIE	You should talk to Silv, Bob.
BOB	It's not a simple as that . . . so leave it, alright?
SILV	He just stood there and watched. I asked him not to laugh . . . but he did. I couldn't stop crying. He couldn't stop laughing. I knew he didn't want to, he just couldn't stop himself.
BOB	She looked so little. Her face was a right mess. Mascara an' that. I used me sleeve to wipe it. Me new suit.
SILV	It mucked it up.
BOB	I wanted to kiss her but I could only bite. I wanted to hold her. But I could only hurt her. She was letting me. She wanted me to . . . too much. I don't kiss.
SILV	Kiss me.
BOB	I don't kiss.
SILV	Please . . .
BOB	She said please . . . me mother used to say please. She was crying 'cos I said, "No, I don't fucking

	kiss, alright?" Me mother used to say please . . . and cry.
SILV	He got real angry and pushed me away.
BOB	She sat there crying, saying she was sorry. It weren't her fault, it were mine . . . don't say sorry . . . MAM! Don't say sorry, it's not your fault . . .
SILV	So I kissed him. Soft, on the lips . . .
BOB	Gentle. I could taste her tears. I wanted her. It would have been easy . . . too easy.
SILV	He didn't want me. He left he his jacket and walked away.
BOB	I went back. I stood across the road. I could hear two cats . . . crying like babies . . . the last train . . . and Silv. Crying. Whimpering like a pup, asking him to stop.
SILV	Jackson allus liked me. I thought I might like him just a bit. He kissed me. I wanted it to be you. He wouldn't get off me. I was frightened. He was heavy . . . too strong. I couldn't stop him. Even though I was crying he wouldn't stop. It was like he wasn't even noticing.
BOB	I wanted to help you. Stop him. I wanted to pull him off. But I couldn't. I kept thinking . . . if it 'ad been me, would I have looked the same as Jackson? Like a dog.
SILV	He finished . . . and he walked away. Your coat was filthy. Stained . . .
BOB	I was gonna run. But then she took off me jacket and was holding it in her arms like a baby . . . like me mam. I remember seeing me mam sat on the bottom of the stairs. She was holding me dad's army jacket . . . with the brass buttons. It was after he left her. I didn't know that, she told

	me he'd been blown to pieces in Ireland. I wish he had. Don't cry mam . . . she still had me . . .
SILV	I was scared to go home. I knew me dad would be waiting up, that look on his face. That look that meant, 'Why?' Why did you have to grow up, why did you have to change? I didn't know what to do, I was cold . . .
BOB	Shivering . . . she couldn't stop. I took me waistcoat off. You can't do that, she said . . . it's your best suit, it all matches . . .
SILV	But I passed him the box. I struck the first one, it was easy. We set fire to his jacket first. Then the waistcoat. Chip papers, anything we could find . . . it was easy . . . beautiful.
BOB	We burnt bus shelter down. We did it together.
SILV	We stood and watched it together. I wasn't frightened no more. I wasn't cold. I felt safe. Bob put his arm around me. Kiss me Bob . . . kiss me.
BOB	But I didn't.
SILV	When they took my baby they asked who the father was. I told them he's a soldier. He's dead, I said . . . blown up in Ireland. I wish he had.
BOB	The night before Valentine's Day me mam burnt everything of me father's. His clothes . . . his shoes . . . even his comb. Everything. Down the garden. It was the biggest fire I'd ever seen. She just stood staring at it. Next day she'd disappeared. Packed up. Gone. I came home from school and nothing. It was as if she'd been a lie . . . a dream. Nothing was left. House was empty. I thought time had tripped . . . got mixed up. I thought she'd come walking in . . . what did it matter? I put me suit on, and went to the disco. I was out of there Monday. Germany. Army. Uniform. Soldier. Right? I was the one leaving, remember? (*Pause*.) Seventeen years and nothing. Then BANG, overnight. She was back in me mind. In me life. BANG, overnight she destroyed

everything. Killed herself. Car. Fire. Fuck knows how. I was glad. He turned up at her funeral pissed. Me father. I allus loved her, he said . . .

(*The lights change. Music plays, the Bee Gee's How Deep Is Your Love, at the wedding reception.* BERNIE *and* RITA, *now fully dressed for the wedding, dance together.* BOB *and* SILV *sit at opposite ends of the room. As the music fades, each is illuminated by a spotlight.*)

RITA Was all like a dream. Head was spinning. Mind was spinning . . . was all like a dream. Nice. Unreal. Real. Dress was on. Veil. Garter. New shoes. New smile. Bigger. Brighter. Smiling inside, outside, all over, all day . . . for the rest of my life. Kiss the bride . . . kiss the bridesmaid?

SILV Why do some things never change . . . was weird to imagine Rita as a bride, wife, married . . . with Bernie. With no reason to want anyone or anything else. The change in her face was unreal, like it was happening but not happening, like it was all a dream . . . I didn't want to spoil her day . . .

BERNIE I'd changed already. I'd changed, there and then. I changed like in a flash, something came alive inside of me. Like in a flash I saw meself different. Bigger. Like I was married now. Wedding. Wife. New life. I had arrived, I was here . . . and the thing was . . . it was exactly where I wanted to be!

(*Music plays, the Bridal March. Blackout.*)